HARVESTING

WILD

LIGHT

Also by Leah Kent

Awakening the Visionary Voice

Intuitive Moon Rituals

Sanctuary

HARVESTING

WILD

LIGHT

LEAH KENT

WILD MOON
press

ISBN 978-1-957234-92-2 (hardcover)
ISBN 978-1-957234-94-6 (paperback)
ISBN 978-1-957234-93-9 (ebook)

Cover and book design by Leah Kent

wildmoonpress.com
WILD MOON
press

For those who speak the green language, and devote themselves to tending the wild edges.

For the witches and story catchers, endlessly weaving the golden tapestry of unbroken threads that bind us in love.

I offer a deep bow of gratitude to our ancestral lands and rooted kin, that hold us and provide the source of all life.

contents

root

Symphytum officinale

intertwined

first the valley called me home
and gifted me with corn and oak,
farm and forest intertwined

then the circle of women gathered,
each body stepping into the ring
one thousand years in the making
I found my place in the coven

rooted, wise, and wild,
sustained in the Ouroboros
of flower, poetry, and rebirth

finding bedrock

granite stones
stand sentinel at the gates
connecting soil and sky

temple and Grandfather
Goddess and root

I feel my breath
steady in their presence

sinking deeper into the ground
my feet find bedrock
and give my heart
permission to float

today

today you will speak
the words on your heart
tattooing them onto
flower petals ready
to hold your story

electric indigo

lick your lips
before you pick up the pen

pinch your cheeks red
and caress your belly

reach for the Earth
draw up big breaths
of indigo electric radiance
pulsing under your feet

fill your lungs with
the intoxication of oxygen
gifted to you by the
meadows, algae, and maples

brush the hairs on your arms
to remember the succulence of truth
before you spill the ink

enough

enough is the hummingbird
drinking sweet nectar
from fringed blossoms

enough is the deep sapphire
eyes fringed with black lashes
of my newborn baby

enough is a fleeting moment
when thoughts settle into
the heartbeat of

yes
okay
breathe
love
receive

pacifica

alone in the Pacific cold
I watch waves gather
on the inky horizon and
wonder which one will
carry me to the broken shells
and seafoam shoreline

I'm never sure if that's what
I want or if my heart would
rather stay here
suspended in the brine
of Earth's amniotic fluid

incarnation

incarnation is trauma
to bring a soul into a body
squeezes and pinches
the infinite awareness
into a too-small container

I wonder if I
will ever fit

story catcher

catch your stories
settle them into the roots
of gentle redwoods

build circles of abalone shells
bare soles blessing
the dappled mossy floor

string words along the
river stones
feeding salmon and sparrow
with prayers of
life and devotion

tapestry

each word is a feather
that fell from the blue
I pick them up and
wonder at their shape

I am mesmerized and afraid
uncertain if my creation
will take flight or
collect dust

each thought is one
string of warp and weft
I go by feel, not knowing
if the pattern will leave me
dazzled or disappointed

slow down love,
she whispers to herself
a gentle lullaby of
wild remembering

find the breeze
and the inner thread of gold
set down the iron will
of self-inflicted judgment

love what emerges
on the loom
without conditions

the long way

drive past the fog
find marker 3.66
walk down the narrow path
until the diamond glint of water
and sounds of mirth enfold you

plunge into the azure cold
bond with the Mother
feel the droplets
of freedom and holy wild
kiss your skin

emerge alive, wet, and bursting
with hunger for days like this
tuck them here and there
to carry and sustain you
long after you leave this portal
and wind your long way home

orchard

I swell to bursting with
the magnetic fragrance of
sticky sour fruit
I pierce each skin with sharp teeth
to see what relief could mean

I stain my fingers and
devour the sweetness
with sighs of delight
and reclaim the right to
dance in this orchard
of my original medicine

I roll each green syllable
over my tongue
liberating an inner well of
elixirs and nectar
that mingle in a starry
field glowing with tranquility

tender heart

what if your tender heart
knew what to say
and precisely how to be understood?

casting circles

read these words so we can
find each other
all the broken daughters
mended with clay and reeds
who glow and flourish despite
the cracks and repairs

wink twice as we pass each
other walking down the street
meeting in the dark fields
of women rising
in wild power
holding hands
casting circles

rest

stitch by stitch
she pieced together
a story laced
with gold
and let her
soft body rest
long enough to
shed the robes
of doubt

fierce

one morning I walked
the forgotten path
beyond silver fields with
frost kissed blades of grass

alone and steady, a flash of instinct
pulled my chin to see her
capture a much needed meal

rabbit or groundhog
sacrificed to a howling
member of the ancient pack

all paws and sharp white teeth
a vulnerable creature
worthy of admiration and respect

I felt the spark of sisterhood
flood my limbs and soften my gaze
how can she carry her wildness
while being judged for doing it wrong?

how does she run fierce in a world
that only permits fake, nice, docile?

feeling my gaze
she ran back to the
dark woods to grieve
together
alone

floating lotus

I carry paper and pen
to a hilltop sanctuary
with a roof of fluttering flags

I settle beside the glassy water
covered in floating lotus blossoms
and sparkling with flashes of gold

I surrender to the devas
letting them move my hand
across the creamy pages
of my cloth bound altar

taking dictation from spirit
marveling at the liberation
that only comes from letting go

restoration

being practical is just
another way to silence
the power you came here
to dedicate to the
restoration of
love on this planet

do not be nice

do not be nice when
you could be a revolution
do not be agreeable when
you could gather women and children
in forests and fields
to beat drums and
write poems on their arms
dedicated to the elements
calling out to Mother Earth
and Father Sky
declaring our devotion
to restoring harmony and honor

do not pretend this isn't happening
when we could work
shoulder to shoulder
making amends and
planting seeds of reparation

binding

we write our words on the page
wishing they will ripple out
to find open ears and
spacious hearts

we speak in whispers to
bind our souls
together in communion
and understanding

we sing our songs never
knowing if they will last
or simply drift away
before settling into some
high nest of a warbler or wren

who will put it back together
and send it out in the morning
across a clear meadow
blanketed in cold morning dew

drink the golden sun

pause
breathe
drink the golden sun
look across the flaming trees
sky dripping with blue
atone for the past
clip the fraying threads
cauterize the veins
meet the woman
urging me
to mourn
without leaving
herself

the woven vessel

I soaked reeds in my bathtub
sliced film negatives
into transparent filaments
of fragmented memory

without plans, I wove a nest
laced with hand-dyed linen
cat gut strings and other
bowerbird treasures

dancing in circles
the pain softened and leapt
from my heart
into the vessel taking shape
in my hands

however we gather the pieces
unraveling is the only way
to reclaim our freedom and
integrate the rewards
of the inner desert

bright light

keep going dear one
this is what they say
rest because this is
decades of work and
we do not wish
for you to burn out
your bright light

alchemy

wander breathe
wonder write
fill the chalice
pour the wine
around the fire

take the medicine
made from poison
be the alchemy
that burns
shrouds of illusion

stretch unfurl
blossom fly
travel on
wind and breath
find
sanctuary

erasing

erase the voice
that told you not to write
or share or shout or protest

erase the line
that kept you bound
stagnating with
creativity, waiting
to burst forth in
a flood of color
splashing on every
surface

navigation

sister. mother. daughter.
sticky trinity of confused belonging
painful love and half-formed tenderness
wild desire and abbreviated nurturing
ancestral tendrils interfering
fractured DNA memories
obscuring connection

girls becoming women
left to navigate alone
a world willing to
sacrifice and steal
their starry wisdom

burning

write like the pen
is on fire and
someone might pull you
away from this
delicious moment of
creative solitude

invisible agreements

speaking the truth
might shatter the
delicate equilibrium
built on invisible agreements

telling the truth might
suffocate the seed
before it takes the first sip
of golden sun

let the truth stay
safe here a while longer

trust yourself to know
when the cauldron is
strong enough to hold
the power
of these words

compass

Calendula officinalis

carry less

carry less
to love more
go into the woods
and leave a trail
of shimmering stardust
that offers the
wildness your love and
infinite oneness

tansy

one summer I met Tansy
bright yellow buttons of ochre
condensed into tight beads of
invisible density
crowning sweet smelling
green leaves dancing
under power lines and
empty fields lined with gravel

her audacity made me smile
her willingness to take root
in rough borders and
shine above the sumac and aster
illuminates my imagination

spark

just when the embers
are cloaked in gray ash
the fire in you burns hotter
they don't know what
secrets and beauty
lay waiting to ignite
at just the
right moment

shedding

let your hand run
headfirst and furious over the
page with freight train
thoughts that don't
stick together
or make sense

because what is sense
except a straight jacket
stitched by a long line of
mothers trying to survive
in a world that demands
silence and whispers

pick apart the seam
with each throaty cry of
pain, bliss, and anguish
shed the tight fitting belts
and leave the concrete walls
to be welcomed back to
the spongy forest floor
of primordial ferns and
wet red bark

come back to the trees
and the antlered stag
who only asks you
to dance and sing

the gatherer

you are the story weaver
mending the tapestry
of a tattered world
separated from Love

you are the gatherer
tracking the lost pieces
scattered by careless hands

you hear the call to
initiate and integrate
the deeper work
of soulful mending

we will not rest until
the healing is bone deep

before the apple

when my soul
longs for the sublime
reunion with the garden
before the apple

I may weep for a moment
offering tears to the
sandstone floor

empty, I look up
and find the constellation
of wild women ready and willing
to share the weight
of rebuilding home

the elders

our future belongs
to the wild hearted women

who keep life flowing
breathing enchantment into rivers
and casting spells in caves

kiss these women
slow down and listen to
the stories they carry

they can tell you the
true measure
of a life well lived

your time is now

become the witch
circle the bonfires
liberate the inner howl
your time is now

hive and circle

we need hive and circle
threshold and portal

we need eyes that hold us
in waves of benevolence

we need starry skies
and the shelter of belonging

we need feet that touch
black fertile soil
and hands that know
what it means to
be whole

heather and meadowsweet

throw your
head back with delight
treasure this
power to breathe
your aliveness
in rhythm with
heather and
meadowsweet

dreaming is a practice

dreaming is a practice
that invites you to
reunite with who you were
before you learned
to be small
quiet
and
obedient

conjuring

can I conjure something from nothing?
would I be able to coax food
from the soil and nibble purple violets
to keep my heart and soul alive

could I move to a forest,
live in a barn filed with baskets
woven from willow, hawthorn, and apple

would I keep a fire lit in the stove
and move slower to let my mind sync
with my body and its wild, gentle wisdom

bridge between worlds

before the Earth called me home
I floated in tropical
waters beneath moonbows
and golden palms

my feet hovered above the ground
as I tried to make my escape
from the mud, blood, and bones
of life in a body

slowly, the trees and flowers
of the green world
brought me back
to my incarnated self

Mugwort and Yarrow,
Comfrey and Birch
sang their songs
until I could see again

until I could inhabit
every limb of this beautiful
bridge between worlds

infinity

thirst quenching light
infinite oceans of vitality
a web of cosmic radiance
that catches you
when you forget

offering

we're all just trying
to find our place in the meadow
our hope is to blossom
and offer our medicine
the root, leaf, and flower
we came here to give

unburdened

if you learned to carry too much
I hope you will consider
putting a few things down

lay them at the feet
of a kind beech tree
with skin smooth bark

she knows what it is
to carry a burden that is
not her own

cleaving

twice my body has
made room for life
I wept with gratitude
never knowing the
loss that would follow
of sanity, sleep, and space

without the sacred Elders
I fumble and trip
in the work of cleaving
my single heart to
hold three flames

every morning I learn
how to be me
in the world we birthed

I yearn to belong to them
without misplacing
my soul
my heartbeat
my voice

the pond

around this pond
the cattails share secrets

they know how long it takes
to rise up from the mud
and make food from buried minerals

they dance and collude
happy to entrust what they know
to those who will listen

in all seasons

I know myself in all seasons
summer sweat and raw hunger
under humid sun storms
cracked skin and hurried work
to tie up loose threads in fall
before the first silent snows

I sleep through short days of winter
allowing the fire of inner vision
to smolder and draw down
instructions from the
numinous compass to
guide the reawakening of spring

elecampane

tucked into a narrow brook
a yellow satellite reaches
between bindweed and mallow
to relay a message of
radiance to the clouds

if you dip your feet
in the cool water
and ask gently
elecampane will help you
shed the false separation
from your own intelligence

soften your gaze
and feel the spiral tighten
towards the center
restoring faith in your
path and purpose
within this collective design

driftwood

steaming summer rains
boiled the creek beds
and overflowed the banks
calm now, I gather
the driftwood bones
piled up to the eroded edges

water knows her true power
reminding us that
life and death are twins
carried in the same cosmic egg

green threads

we need our shadows
our graceful second skins
we need respite
from the exposure of
full bright sun

this sweet moss tells stories
from the darkest places
where root, rock, and
invisible threads
hold the world together

laurel

blooming mountain laurel showered
the path with conch shell pink petals
that one wet June when
I could no longer wait
to recover my wild soul

each shrub cried out
her exuberant welcoming
glimmering dewdrops
of celebration for
this threshold crossed

amethyst

dance your way down
the amethyst stream
past the queen of the meadow
and the nuthatch nest

sit upon the time worn fieldstone
find the drumbeat in your chest
breathing words longing to be spoken

carry them to the next fallow field
waiting to be treasured
by the wide-eyed girl
looking for a sign that
her voice is welcomed here

big river

in the elbow of the big river
where salt meets fresh water
I shed my selkie skin
trading innocence for passion
releasing safety to embody wonder

I carry that water with me
sipping with closed eyes of reverence
grateful for the courage
of that hot-blooded creature I once was

I love her for walking away
untying all the strings
designed to tether her to the garden gate

I love her for abandoning the path
that would have dried her out
and divided her from the
dew-soaked horizon
that belongs only to her

spring ephemeral

ephemeral reminders that spring
only comes once a year
bloodroot cohosh wild ginger
daring to show themselves
each and every time the portal swings open

deep below the rhizomes whisper and plan
gathering all that's needed
to turn sunlight into the softest petals
of linen white, blue, and crimson

fed by waterfalls and snow melt
the forest floor shares
these hidden beauties
if only you know where to look

dissolution

never underestimate
the power of water to tear
down your walls
and in the dissolution
to find sweetness and relief

circle

Solidago canadensis

wings

just because your wings
have no feathers doesn't
mean you're bereft of the
power to soar, fly, and
embrace the horizon

born hungry

my heart was born hungry
for solitude and empty hours
when I could dream of rooms
that turned into gardens
and drive my car straight
to the Moon

my heart came here heavy
resolutely determined to shed
these snakeskin layers
and alchemize them into
glimmering cabochons of light
for others to find

resilience

resilience is picking up the pen
every morning and every sunset
married to my own voice
in times of ease and again
when I am shattered

remembering

when was the last time
you played with kelp
or crowned yourself
with cucumber scented
lake grasses

decorating your shoulders
with plump green gems
patiently waiting to be
remembered and befriended

listening

writing at night was always
the only way to hear
what my wildest
dreams wanted to be

untangling

some mornings the voice that
keeps you quiet and hidden
is too loud
drink more coffee
bang pots and pans
write faster and
shake the fear loose
minutes are too precious
to stay tangled in barbed wire
opinions that never belonged
to you anyway

answering the call

luminous green world filled with promise
beyond curtains of trumpet vine and grape
hide the stinging secrets of nettle and goldthread

these delicate mysteries carry medicine
for skin that always feels too thin, too raw

I heard the call and answered to make beauty
and peace from weeds and brambles

april

releasing
the deepest exhale
letting the Earth wrap and cradle me
soft pupils and raspberry flowers
tasting the unveiled ripeness
of April dawn

choose again

body paint and bronze hoops
ritual robes for the ink black ceremony

each day we choose again
who we are and who we speak for

how we will be the revolution
or uphold the symptoms of our
grief
self-abandonment
separation

let the circle of elders call you
to the sacred center
a compass of
fire and belonging
truth and restoration

taproot

plant your taproot deeply, my love
anchor yourself in this wild place
cast your net wide to draw forth all
that you need and drink it in
without shame or apology

riding sundown

we wait too long because we
can't bear the thought of
breaking the spell and
puncturing the membrane
of this perfect moment

harmonious and free
the skin dissipates anyway
whether we like it or not
our real work is to gently
ride the descending
wave of sundown

all we can do then is hold each
other close, wrapped in warm
towels and loving arms
washing the day away,
going gently to sleep
waiting to do it again

softer this time, worn
around the edges,
sweet and pink like
rose petals in July

threshold

embody your wisdom
publish your gems of insight
share the truth you've earned
be the wisdom keeper
who puts out her hand
and guides others
across the threshold
your magic must not
be lost or forgotten

the bramble

woven through redwood roads are
endless miles of blackberry brambles
one summer I found them, perfectly ripe
plump and warm, hanging on every tendril

with hats and bags scavenged from
tight spaces underneath the seats
we picked and ate our way through
thorns and bees, burning our necks
and crosshatching our skin

I took them home and baked them
nestled below butter, sugar, and oats
I remember slipping them into the oven
setting the timer and waiting

each bite brought me back to my body
a holy communion between womb and fruit
berry and breast

I carry this with me, the instructions
for how to merge with her, honor her
how to receive her sacred gifts
of sweet, sour, bitter, salty
earth, wood, fire, water

uncensored

remember that being nice will always be
a fluttering moth who censors your brilliance

being nice serves only them while watering
down the divine awakening of your
luminous heart

crescent hours

keep close to the crescent hours
when sun and moon dip
soft light below the sea and mountains
listen for quiet breezes
carrying poems or colors
imprinted with an atlas
for your weathered heart
to follow

the last woman in the lake

I want to be the last woman in the lake
so I can finally be alone with the warm water
and watch a Moon rise over the Seven Sisters
magic light dances on my beaded skin the
sparkles taste sweet and glimmer on my tongue

how many soul stars have danced here before me
casting wishes into moonbeam waves
and sending sweet songs from here
to the far shore

blaze

lover
creature
fire
there has always been a blaze within me
even as I tried to stamp out the flames
and hide from the red fingers
the light always bursts
from the seams

I'm wiser now and know
to tend the bonfire
with reverence and open arms
before the smoldering coals
catch fire and spread in the
most inconvenient circumstances

so I tend the inner hearth
marveling at my own raw power

stoking the embers with
awe and admiration

threaded to the sun

your heart is
threaded to the sun
in a tapestry of gold

each strand of light
you wrap around
yourself is stitched
with your infinite
radiance

jade coat

in a dream I saw her
gliding through the forest
as if she had wings on her heels
that lifted her off the ground
in a jade velvet coat
hair woven and threaded
with grass and petals, I followed
her deeper into the dark heart
of thick air and pulsing life

she showed me the well
gilded and glowing
a spring of alchemy and magic
that was always meant for me

I kept it hidden all those years
preserving its power to be
unbound at this precise moment

intoxication

anything is possible
when bathed in milky moonlight
submerged in the flowing darkness
sound amplifies and symbols float
across the screen of inner sight

the unknown comes close
brushing against your skin with
intoxicating pulses of soothing clarity

you can almost trace the map
of dark pathways from here
to the ancient grove of your
truest desires at midnight
you always know the way

the canyon

I am the streambed
not the water
I am the channel who
gathers the rain
focusing the power of
life's elixir and
carrying it down
the hills and canyons
to the parched meadow
and salty shore

tend to my edges
let the roots below me
drink what they will

do not interfere with
the harmonious balance
of giving and receiving
love me without restraint
and you will always
have what is needed
to quench your true thirst

where flowers shine

I closed my eyes this morning
and saw an amber firefly
falling and glowing inside my eyelid
a single shooting star across
my very own horizon

maybe it was an echo
from the spotlight in the room,
but I like to think it was a
petal of marigold or poppy
inviting me to leave the chores behind
and come back to a place
where flowers shine in the darkness

cauldron

writing is all in the hips
the words steep in a pelvic cauldron
simmering together with
fragrant herbs
circling stems of thyme
finding each other
forming sacred alliances
while the bones sink to
the bottom

settling

gripped by sand, water, needle, and cloud
I let summer touch my thirsty skin
all the swirls of care and worry
buzz in my body before finding
a way to settle and unfold

the white pines dance as the
bald eage banks
diving so close I could
reach her gleaming feathers

being a child of the Pacific, it feels exotic
to befriend these eastern freshwater lakes
learning their beauty and
breaking the code that tells me
when gray thunderclouds will roll in

yet here I am, finding and making a home
sustained by tenacious hope
and the willingness to
receive this land's embrace

unwind here

as autumn tumbles and crashes
over summer, I strain to catch the last
stand of primrose and the waning
clutch of black eyed susan

the shock of finding them
amidst the blackened milkweed
catches a sigh in my throat
as I reach out to crush their
yellow petals straight into my heart
hoping to keep them
here just a few days longer

I need their supple brilliance
to burn through the long winter
I want them to unwind here
sheltered from the snow
in the pulsing heat of this body

portal

Dipsacus fullonum

carrying diamonds

I write to find myself again and again
to carve pathways of truth with
skin and bone and blood and earth

I write in layers
onion skin thin
faint and translucent
building over time until I can see
the density of me
the messy fullness
and yearnings of unbridled desire

I carry these diamonds in unlikely places
a back pocket, a woven basket in a sunny field
I keep my priceless treasure
hiding in plain view
illuminated by the sun

a voice reminds me to check
that pocket and touch this raw
loving power a voice that invites me
to expand the boundaries of what
I allow myself to be

sand and stone

sand and stone have always been
the only element
to hold space for my fire

fierce enough to contain
the endless blaze of
creative flames I was
born to carry

lionheart

Motherwort hid behind the town sign
hoping to go unnoticed, unmarked
letting her work her magic
quietly, surreptitiously
a few hollow stems lending their
feral power to enchant the margins
between machines and the wild
sanctuaries of bird songs

still, I asked for permission
and felt or wished for her yes
I pulled her up gently by the root
and tucked her, muddy and naked,
into the brown grocery bag

I placed her in the front garden
with a prayer of ancestral gratitude
I left her with sisters, yarrow, alchemilla, indigo
the rains came all summer and
I imagined her strong roots beneath black soil
searching and wondering where they had landed

I hope she is happy there
I hope I am a worthy gardener

what we know

we never know if we're good
we only know if we're here
fully enchanted with
sunsets and wildflowers

we only know how to plant
seeds and carry water
while our bodies coax us forward
with endless desire
and infinite love of the magic
that was already here

innocent crocus and curious daffodils
a riot of color and a tangle of green
tells me the world is good
and the time has come
to stop trying so hard

goldenrod gone by

in the waning days
when light slips below horizon
we soak up every ray of warmth
tracing woodland trails
seeking pools of sun

amidst the goldenrod gone by
I find brave flowers
who found an oasis of heat and light
a family of red clover
a single spark of wild blue chicory
a last head of white yarrow

the flowers hug the path's edge
stretching the season and reminding
us to spiral ourselves all the way
in to rest in the haven
of our innermost song

let summer's gifts integrate, solidify,
and organize themselves into tapestries
of knowledge and wisdom

we can be quiet now, and wait

beacon

be a beacon
a light in the darkness
that gathers moths together

let one flickering ember
kiss the wick of your beeswax candle
hold the glow over the page and portal

trace your finger over the veins
of this map you were born with
and soak in the creamy velvet of skin

luminaria

luminaria in the garden
children lay cedar branches
and pine bundles on frozen grass
around and around, they meet one another
at the oak stump in the center

step by tender step they carry
their paper lanterns, suspended
from silver wire

steady, reverent, uncertain
they walk with gazes fixed down
guided by tree spirits
knowing exactly where to place the left
foot and then the right

around the spiral the mothers and fathers sing
of geese migrating and soul flames
that glow in Winter

trees hum beneath us
they gave their limbs for this ritual
hoping we will remember our kinship
wishing for some of us to
bless the earth with more of these
bright solstice melodies

where we belong

I belong where I am
born beneath redwoods that
disappear into the sky
and grassy headlands
falling into the sea

I belong where I am
called to wild nettle patches
and towering white pines
carrying messages
to the stars

softer

do not be afraid to aim higher
the softer you become,
the more joy and radiance you
can experience

sway
let go
dance

be the conduit and
cast off what weighs you down
receive with a wide open heart
without losing your anchors
in the sacred ground

echo

ice cold nights always come
paving the way for a barred owl's call
to echo through bare trees

the raucous carnival of summer gardens
will droop and fall softly to the Earth
flowers will retreat
drawing their sugars into the soil

I will hold vigil for the Sun
my life orbiting around the hearth
burning candles and stirring the soup
to stay closer than ever
to the brilliant light within

mirrors

flower women need
tribe, hive, and circle
we need mirrors
carved from smooth stone
and sweet honeysuckle

we need trees and streams
that reflect who we are
who we came from
what we are here to become

flower women draw close together
around mandalas of leaves and petals
foreheads touching in reverence
prayer and shared belonging

step in
we say
and join our temple

breathe slow
we say
and find your place here

ash and cedar

when I come to the forest alone
the trees greet me with wordless grace

when I come to the forest alone
I make up songs and sing them
to the ash and cedar
pressing my spine into the
ridges and folds of their skin

I come here to know what I believe
and witness the soul of the land
I stop, remember, and re-enter
my wild haven

I can breathe again
close my eyes
and hear the call
of moss covered voices

when you exhale

when you exhale
silver stars form in the sky

when you weep, wide rivers
fill up with your wisdom

when you close your eyes
a weary world rests and knows
it is loved by you

mystery

gaze into the blossoming poppy and
the voice will call to you

reach your arms up to the moonlit sky
and let the guidance you seek
pour into your fingertips

let the breeze share its secrets
entrusting you with a code that unlocks
the mysteries of the sacred
ground within you

tending the wheel

I can smell the moss
blanketing a fallen birch beside
the swift cold brook

we bring our summer gifts
passing petals and herbs
from one hand to another

rose and calendula
dance with sage and mallow
as I cast them into the water

time cracks open
in these shaded woods
as my body remembers these
same motions and sisterhoods
lifetime after lifetime

we plant seeds of medicine
tend the flowers
harvest the bounty
and return it all to the soil

tending the wheel
belonging to the liminal space
where wild meets woman

grandmothers

what if everyday
I took my own medicine
and brought gifts to
the Mother Oak
who grows on the hill
and I asked for help
not because I am weak
but because I am strong
and willing to let my heart soften

what if I reunited with the Goddesses of
my grandmothers and called them by name,
Gabija, Brigid, Nerthus
keepers of hearth and fire
fertility and freedom
welcoming them at every dawn
and again at every dusk
to teach me what they've always known

the loom

we are the faceted
treasures of the divine

weavers of secrets
that have always belonged
to the mystics, visionaries, and poets

find the place in your own
heart that ties into the
warp and weft of these storylines

come closer to the loom
to study the sacred geometry
of how we fit together

over and under
around and through
rhythm and wonder

drawing the light of the cosmos
down into these woolen
threads to sparkle
under the stars

rays

I never knew
that each thing I
called a helianthus petal
burning yellow
and magnetic to bees
raising its face
in greeting to the sun
was a whole and complete
flower
a ray connected
by invisible life
to a fertile seed

vitality

when the time comes
embrace the primal urge
to draw your vital force
deep into the roots

spirals of gold and plum
coming in from the cold
to find sacred shelter

feed yourself first

feed yourself first
crimson rosehips and slippery kelp
pick the freshest serrated leaves
from dandelion covered hills
gather velvet dappled petals
and the newly emerging
viridescent tips of the last
standing hemlocks
merging your body
with the sun
in a spinning tale
of infinite love

wild roses

we cannot lose
the lusciousness of being alive
warming our bodies on a coastline
of sparkling sand or kissing
the salty lips of your beloved

we cannot let go
of wild summer roses
pricking our fingers as
the smell of desire hangs
so thick in the air

we cannot be separated from
the water that pulses
in our veins mixed with
blood and wild magic

metamorphosis

nothing can evade the primal force
of constant change and metamorphosis
our cosmic invitation is to find
the gift in the unfurling

the portal

yesterday I placed a triangle of slate
at her feet where bark meets loam
a portal opens where mystery
can wind between lower and upper worlds

I hum and retrace the path
taking form between cedar roots
and wild ginger

feet on earth
hand on hemlock bough
twin hearts
beating at dawn

invocation

welcome the ungraspable medicine
encoded in each strand of a spider's web
suspended in a single drop of winter rain

close your eyes when you hear the call
to navigate the darkness
and invoke the power of each element

air my breath
water my blood
earth my body
fire my soul

protection

yarrow offers us a shield
an umbel of clustered blossoms
a flower with one thousand leaves

she teaches us that our vitality
relies on healthy boundaries
that our empathic souls require fierce protection

she draws iron up from the soil
each inflorescence blushing with ferrous dye

listen to her chanting
your strength is your beauty
root down to rise

labyrinth

you can feel the spiral
alive in your lungs
animating your heart

winding your way deep
towards the center where
the air is black

fingers read the cold ground
to find the single thread
that knows the way back

pick it up
the mist urges
and with every step
I will help you

return to the
wild light

carried away

may this veil be lifted

may these worn out beliefs
tumble away on the wind

may these sorrows and grudges
be carried away with
the sunset over the ridgeline

may radiance, joy, and love
be welcomed into my life
rising in the East with the
Sun every morning

the initiate

I sit at the feet of my teachers
tendrils snaking underground
in networks of weeds
wild flowers and bitter herbs

a rich humus absorbs
my lingering doubts
so I may be
a hollow bone

channel your medicine
beloved one
and share these
unearthed gems

let the light in

make space
let go
let the light in
be the witch
be the magician
be the one
your heart has
always desired

Achillea millefolium

gratitude

With deep reverence, I acknowledge that I live and work in unceded Pocumtuc land.

I offer these words within a deep commitment to create a more diverse, equitable, and inclusive community in which people of different ethnicities, genders, cultures, belief systems, class backgrounds, ages, abilities, and sexual orientations have genuine and equal opportunities to thrive.

At each step of my rewilding, I have been supported and loved by countless kindred spirits, who have each contributed to the unfurling of this book.

I am endlessly grateful to the women in my life who have offered their love of language and the wild throughout my life. Natalie, my grandmother who taught me, among many things, to eat wild sorrel and the proper usage of who and whom. My literature teachers in high school, Sarah and Bronwyn, who encouraged me to think more radically and express myself with conviction and power. Elaina, my sister, lifelong co-conspirator and editor, who flew across the country to talk to flowers and sing with me.

I have had the pleasure of studying different facets of herbalism and flower essences with an incredible circle of women, and each has played a sacred role in my green initiation. I honor the women of Woodland Essence, Heartsong Farm, Sweet Birch Herbals, Milk & Honey Herbs, and Her Wild Roots for offering accessible and open-hearted ways to see the gifts being offered all around us.

I offer a deep bow of gratitude to Brooke and her Wild Temple school for modeling a form of rooted wisdom that brings so much radiant healing into this world.

I am forever grateful to each of these women for their profound transmissions of the green language, and sharing their knowledge with generosity and light.

I honor my ancestors, whose ingenuity, resilience and determination made my existence and work possible.

From the bottom of my heart, I am grateful to the wild men in my life, my partner and our beloved sons, for the love and joy they bring into the world.

about the author

Leah Kent is a writer and book coach who helps wisdom keepers and visionaries write and publish transformational books about their work in the world. She is the creator of the Wild Embodied Writing method, and the author of *Awakening the Visionary Voice*, *Intuitive Moon Rituals*, and *Sanctuary*.

A native of California, Leah now lives in Western Massachusetts. When not writing, she's slowly building an off-grid oasis amidst the maples and cedars in her family's beautiful forest in Northeastern Vermont.

Connect with Leah:
leahkent.net
instagram.com/leahkentco
Substack: Wild Embodied Writing